To

_____

From

_____

Date

_____

© 2010 Summerside Press™
Minneapolis 55438
www.summersidepress.com
Promises and Blessings for Mothers
A *Pocket Inspirations* Book

ISBN 978-1-935416-93-7

Scripture references are from the following sources: The Holy
Bible, New International Version®, NIV®. Copyright © 1973, 1978,
1984 by Biblica, Inc.™ Used by permission of Zondervan. All rights
reserved worldwide. The New King James Version (NKJV). Copyright
© 1982 by Thomas Nelson, Inc. Used by permission. The Holy Bible,
New Living Translation® (NLT). Copyright © 1996, 2004. Used by
permission of Tyndale House Publishers, Inc., Wheaton, Illinois
60189. *The Message* © 1993, 1994, 1995, 1996, 2000, 2001, 2002 by
Eugene Peterson. Used by permission of NavPress, Colorado Springs,
CO. The New Century Version® (NCV). Copyright © 1987, 1988, 1991
by Thomas Nelson, Inc. Used by permission. All rights reserved.

Compiled by Barbara Farmer
Designed by Jeff and Lisa Franke

*Summerside Press™ is an inspirational publisher offering fresh,
irresistible books to uplift the heart and engage the mind.*

Printed in the USA.

PROMISES & BLESSINGS
FOR A
Mother's
HEART

Pi Pocket
INSPIRATIONS

summerside
PRESS

The Beauty of Motherhood

Most of all the other beautiful things in life
come by twos and threes, by dozens and
hundreds. Plenty of roses, stars, sunsets,
rainbows, brothers and sisters, aunts
and cousins, comrades and friends—
but only one mother in the whole world.

KATE DOUGLAS WIGGIN

Ask any four-year-old boy, "Who's
the most beautiful woman in the world?"
His mommy! Ask any grown daughter
caring for her aging mother the same
question, and you'll get the same answer....
Moms spend a lifetime humbling
themselves in taking care of others.
Nothing is more attractive.

LISA WHELCHEL

For attractive lips,
Speak words of kindness.
For lovely eyes,
Seek out the good in people.
For a slim figure,
Share your food with the hungry.
For beautiful hair,
Let a child run his or her fingers
through it once a day.
For poise,
Walk with the knowledge
you'll never walk alone.

AUDREY HEPBURN

To be a child is to know the joy of living.
To have a child is to know the beauty of life.

....

Therefore, as God's chosen people, holy and dearly loved, clothe yourselves with compassion, kindness, humility, gentleness and patience.

COLOSSIANS 3:12 NIV

....

The Wonder of Wisdom

For the wisdom of the wisest being God has made
ends in wonder; and there is nothing on earth
so wonderful as the budding soul of a little child.

LUCY LARCOM

A fiery sunset, tiny pansies by the wayside,
the sound of raindrops tapping on the roof—
what extraordinary delight we find in the simple
wonders of life! With wide eyes and full hearts,
we may cherish what others often miss.

....

*I am convinced beyond a shadow
of any doubt that the most valuable pursuit
we can embark upon is to know God.*

KAY ARTHUR

....

All things bright and beautiful,
All creatures great and small,
All things wise and wonderful,
The Lord God made them all.

CECIL FRANCES ALEXANDER

A wise gardener plants his seeds, then has
the good sense not to dig them up every few
days to see if a crop is on the way. Likewise,
we must be patient as God brings the answers...
in His own good time.

QUIN SHERRER

A child's hand in yours—what tenderness
and power it arouses. You are instantly the very
touchstone of wisdom and strength.

MARJORIE HOLMES

What a wildly wonderful world, GOD! You
made it all, with Wisdom at your side, made
earth overflow with your wonderful creations.

PSALM 104:24 THE MESSAGE

A Heart Full of Joy

Our hearts were made for joy. Our hearts were
made to enjoy the One who created them.
Too deeply planted to be much affected by
the ups and downs of life, this joy is a knowing
and a being known by our Creator.
He sets our hearts alight with radiant joy.

WENDY MOORE

Joy is warm and radiant and clamors
for expressions and experience.

DOROTHY SEGOVIA

If one is joyful, it means that one is faithfully
living for God, and that nothing else counts; and
if one gives joy to others one is doing God's work.
With joy without and joy within, all is well.

JANET ERSKINE STUART

All who seek the LORD will praise him.
Their hearts will rejoice with everlasting joy.

PSALM 22:26 NLT

As we grow in our capacities to see and enjoy
the joys that God has placed in our lives,
life becomes a glorious experience of
discovering His endless wonders.

Since you get more joy out of giving joy to others,
you should put a good deal of thought into
the happiness that you are able to give.

ELEANOR ROOSEVELT

....

*When hands reach out in friendship,
hearts are touched with joy.*

....

The Truth in Love

Love never gives up.
Love cares more for others than for self.
Love doesn't want what it doesn't have.
Love doesn't strut,
Doesn't have a swelled head,
Doesn't force itself on others,
Isn't always "me first,"
Doesn't fly off the handle,
Doesn't keep score of the sins of others,
Doesn't revel when others grovel,
Takes pleasure in the flowering of truth,
Puts up with anything,
Trusts God always,
Always looks for the best,
Never looks back,
But keeps going to the end.

1 CORINTHIANS 13:4–7 THE MESSAGE

Love. No greater theme can be emphasized.
No stronger message can be proclaimed. No finer
song can be sung. No better truth can be imagined.

CHARLES SWINDOLL

I wish you peace—in the world in which you live
and in the smallest corner of the heart
where truth is kept. I wish you faith—
to help define your living and your life.
More I cannot wish you—except perhaps love—
to make all the rest worthwhile.

ROBERT A. WARD

Amid ancient lore the Word of God stands
unique and pre-eminent. Wonderful in its
construction, admirable in its adaptation,
it contains truths that a child may comprehend,
and mysteries into which angels desire to look.

FRANCES ELLEN WATKINS HARPER

*The deepest truth blooms only
from the deepest love.*

HEINRICH HEINE

To Live, Laugh, and Love

Whole-hearted, ready laughter heals,
encourages, relaxes anyone within hearing
distance. The laughter that springs from love
makes wide the space around—
gives room for the loved one to enter in.

EUGENIA PRICE

People can be divided into three groups:
Those who make things happen,
those who watch things happen, and
those who wonder what happened.

....

Take time to laugh. It is the music of the soul.

....

Today's Forecast: Partly rational with brief
periods of coherent thought giving way
to complete apathy by tonight.

SHERRIE WEAVER

If you can learn to laugh in spite of the
circumstances that surround you, you will
enrich others, enrich yourself, and
more than that, you will last!

BARBARA JOHNSON

If it weren't for the last minute,
nothing would get done.

If you can remain calm,
you just don't have all the facts.

The best laughter, the laughter that can heal,
the laughter that has the truest ring, is the laughter
that flowers out of a love for life and its Giver.

MAXINE HANCOCK

Let all those who seek You
rejoice and be glad in You.

PSALM 40:16 NKJV

A good laugh is as good as a prayer sometimes.

LUCY MAUD MONTGOMERY

A Quiet Time

We need quiet time to examine our lives
openly and honestly....
Spending quiet time alone gives your mind
an opportunity to renew itself and create order.

SUSAN L. TAYLOR

If a care is too small to be turned into a prayer
then it is too small to be made into a burden.

I give you thanks, O LORD, with all my heart...
As soon as I pray, you answer me;
you encourage me by giving me strength.

PSALM 138:1, 3 NLT

Open wide the windows of our spirits and fill us
full of light; open wide the door of our hearts
that we may receive and entertain Thee
with all the powers of our adoration.

CHRISTINA ROSSETTI

We must take our troubles to the Lord,
but we must do more than that;
we must leave them there.

HANNAH WHITALL SMITH

Whate'er the care which breaks thy rest,
Whate'er the wish that swells thy breast;
Spread before God that wish, that care,
And change anxiety to prayer.

....

*You pay God a compliment by
asking great things of Him.*

TERESA OF AVILA

....

Always be joyful. Pray continually,
and give thanks whatever happens.
That is what God wants for you in Christ Jesus.

1 THESSALONIANS 5:16-18 NCV

Do All You Can

Not everyone possesses boundless energy
or a conspicuous talent. We are not equally
blessed with great intellect or physical beauty
or emotional strength. But we have all been
given the same ability to be faithful.

GIGI GRAHAM TCHIVIDJIAN

Do all the good you can
By all the means you can
In all the ways you can
In all the places you can
To all the people you can
As long as ever you can.

JOHN WESLEY

No one can arrive from being
talented alone. God gives talent,
work transforms talent into genius.

ANNA PAVLOVA

The strength of a person consists in finding
out the way God is going and going that way.

HENRY WARD BEECHER

Have a purpose in life, and having it,
throw into your work such strength of mind
and muscle as God has given you.

THOMAS CARLYLE

....

*If your lips can speak a word of encouragement
to a weary soul, you have a talent.*

EVA J. CUMMINGS

....

Whatever you do, whether in word or deed,
do it all in the name of the Lord Jesus,
giving thanks to God the Father through him.

COLOSSIANS 3:17 NIV

The Simplicity of Childhood

It is the little things that count
And give a mother pleasure—
The things her children bring to her
Which they so richly treasure...
The picture that is smudged a bit
With tiny fingerprints,
The colored rock, the lightning bugs,
The sticky peppermints;
The ragged, bright bouquet of flowers
A child brings, roots and all—
These things delight a mother's heart
Although they seem quite small.
A mother can see beauty
In the very smallest thing
For there's a little bit of heaven
In a small child's offering.

KATHERINE NELSON DAVIS

With our children who thrive on simple pleasures,
our work and our entire society can be renewed.

SARA WENGER SHENK

My childhood home was the home
of a woman with a genius for
inventing daily life, who found happiness
in the simplest of gestures.

LAURA FRONTY

"Unless you accept God's kingdom in the
simplicity of a child, you'll never get in."
Then, gathering the children up in his arms,
[Jesus] laid his hands of blessing on them.

MARK 10:15-16 THE MESSAGE

....

*The incredible gift of the ordinary!
Glory comes streaming from
the table of daily life.*

MACRINA WIEDERKEHR

....

All Creation Sings

It is an extraordinary and beautiful thing that God,
in creation...works with the beauty of matter;
the reality of things; the discoveries of the senses,
all five of them; so that we, in turn,
may hear the grass growing;
see a face springing to life in love and laughter....
The offerings of creation...
our glimpses of truth.

MADELEINE L'ENGLE

....

Let there be many windows in your soul,
That all the glory of the universe may beautify it.

ELLA WHEELER WILCOX

....

It is always wise to stop wishing for things
long enough to enjoy the fragrance
of those now flowering.

PATRICE GIFFORD

In all ranks of life the human heart yearns for the
beautiful, and the beautiful things that God
makes are His gift to all alike.

HARRIET BEECHER STOWE

Every good action and
every perfect gift is from God.
These good gifts come down
from the Creator of the sun, moon, and stars,
who does not change
like their shifting shadows.
God decided to give us life
through the word of truth
so we might be the most important
of all the things he made.

JAMES 1:17–18 NCV

Loving Creator, help me reawaken my childlike
sense of wonder at the delights of Your world!

MARILYN MORGAN HELLEBERG

Living in the Present

Normal day, let me be aware of
the treasure you are. Let me learn from you,
love you, bless you before you depart.
Let me not pass you by in quest of some
rare and perfect tomorrow.

Women of adventure have conquered their fates
and know how to live exciting and fulfilling
lives right where they are. They have learned
to reinvent themselves and find creative ways
to enjoy the world and their place in it.
They know how to take mini-vacations,
stop and smell the roses, and
live fully in the moment.

BARBARA JENKINS

If you surrender completely to the moments
as they pass, you live more richly those moments.

ANNE MORROW LINDBERGH

Let the day suffice, with all its joys and failings,
its little triumphs and defeats.... Happily, if sleepily,
welcome evening as a time of rest, and let it
slip away, losing nothing.

KATHLEEN NORRIS

For I have learned in whatever state I am, to be
content. I know what it is to be in need, and I know
what it is to have plenty. I have learned the secret
of being content in any and every situation,
whether well fed or hungry, whether
living in plenty or in want.

PHILIPPIANS 4:11–12 NIV

....

*Children have neither past nor future; they
enjoy the present, which very few of us do.*

JEAN DE LA BRUYÉRE

....

What Children Want

Children will not remember you
for the material things you provided,
but for the feeling that you cherished them.

GAIL GRENIER SWEET

They might not need me; but they might.
I'll let my head be just in sight;
A smile as small as mine might be
Precisely their necessity.

EMILY DICKINSON

Tradition is a form of promise from parent to child.
It's a way to say, "I love you," "I'm here for you,"
and "Some things will not change."

LYNN LUDWICK

....

*The everlasting God is your place of safety,
and his arms will hold you up forever.*

DEUTERONOMY 33:27 NCV

....

The very word "motherhood"
has an emotional depth and significance
few terms have. It bespeaks nourishment
and safety and sheltering arms.

MARJORIE HOLMES

A mother is a person who, seeing there are only
four pieces of pie for five people, promptly
announces she never did care for pie.

TENNEVA JORDAN

She is their earth....
She is their food and their bed and the
extra blanket when it grows cold in the night;
she is their warmth and their health
and their shelter.

KATHERINE BUTLER HATHAWAY

His Promised Attention

See each morning a world made anew,
as if it were the morning of the very
first day;...treasure and use it,
as if it were the final hour
of the very last day.

FAY HARTZELL ARNOLD

This is the real gift: you have been given
the breath of life, designed with a unique,
one-of-a-kind soul that exists forever—the way
that you choose to live it doesn't change
the fact that you've been given the gift of *being*
now and forever. Priceless in value, you are
handcrafted by God, who has a personal
design and plan for each of us.

WENDY MOORE

The God who created, names, and numbers
the stars in the heavens also numbers the
hairs of my head.... He pays attention to very
big things and to very small ones. What matters
to me matters to Him, and that changes my life.

ELISABETH ELLIOT

*The greatest gift we can give one another is
rapt attention to one another's existence.*

SUE ATCHLEY EBAUGH

Store up for yourselves treasures in heaven,
where moth and rust do not destroy, and where
thieves do not break in and steal. For where
your treasure is, there your heart will be also.

MATTHEW 6:20-21 NIV

The Heritage of Children

We live in the present, we dream of the future,
but we learn eternal truths from the past.

LUCY MAUD MONTGOMERY

Every material goal, even if it is met, will pass
away. But the heritage of children is timeless.
Our children are our messages to the future.

BILLY GRAHAM

I will sing of the mercies of the LORD forever;
With my mouth will I make known
Your faithfulness to all generations.

PSALM 89:1 NKJV

There is nothing quite so deeply satisfying as the
solidarity of a family united across the generations
and miles by a common faith and history.

SARA WENGER SHENK

Life is no brief candle to me.
It is a...splendid torch...and I want to make it
burn as brightly as possible before handing
it over to future generations.

GEORGE BERNARD SHAW

Favorite people, favorite places,
favorite memories of the past ...
These are the joys of a lifetime...
these are the things that last.

Father, help me to take the time to create stories
with my children. May good memories hold
the generations together. Amen.

SCOTT WALKER

....

In every child is planted
the seed of a great future.

....

Loved by God

Blessed be the God and Father of our Lord
Jesus Christ, the Father of mercies and God
of all comfort, who comforts us in all our
tribulation, that we may be able to comfort those
who are in any trouble, with the comfort with
which we ourselves are comforted by God.

2 CORINTHIANS 1:3-4 NKJV

As a rose fills a room with its fragrance,
so will God's love fill our lives.

MARGARET BROWNLEY

God is every moment totally aware of each
one of us. Totally aware in intense
concentration and love.... No one passes
through any area of life, happy or tragic,
without the attention of God.

EUGENIA PRICE

The treasure our heart searches for
is found in the ocean of God's love.

JANET WEAVER SMITH

Before anything else, above all else,
beyond everything else, God loves us.
God loves us extravagantly,
ridiculously, without limit or condition.
God is in love with us...
God yearns for us.

ROBERTA BONDI

....
*Whoever walks toward God one step,
God runs toward him two.*

JEWISH PROVERB
....

Stand outside this evening. Look at the stars.
Know that you are special and loved by
the One who created them.

Mother and Child

There is no other closeness in human life
like the closeness between a mother and
her baby—chronologically, physically,
and spiritually they are just a few heartbeats
away from being the same person.

SUSAN CHEVER

....

*A mother's arms are made of tenderness
and children sleep soundly in them.*

VICTOR HUGO

....

No joy in nature is so sublimely
affecting as the joy of a mother at the
good fortune of her child.

JEAN PAUL RICHTER

The mother's heart is the child's schoolroom.

HENRY WARD BEECHER

She is clothed with strength and dignity,
and she laughs without fear of the future.
When she speaks, her words are wise,
and she gives instructions with kindness.
She carefully watches everything in her
household and suffers nothing from laziness.
Her children stand and bless her.

PROVERBS 31:25–28 NLT

Children are the anchors that hold a mother to life.

SOPHOCLES

All mothers are rich
when they love their children....
Their love is always the most beautiful of joys.

MAURICE MAETERLINCK

There is an enduring tenderness in the love
of a mother to a [child] that transcends
all other affections of the heart.

WASHINGTON IRVING

Promised Dividends

Choices can change our lives profoundly.
The choice to mend a broken relationship,
to say yes to a difficult assignment, to lay aside
some important work to play with a child,
to visit some forgotten person—
these small choices may affect our lives eternally.

GLORIA GAITHER

Let your light shine before men,
that they may see your good deeds
and praise your Father in heaven.

MATTHEW 5:16 NIV

....

Invest in people rather than things
for herein lies eternal dividends.

....

Can you measure the worth of a sunbeam,
The worth of a treasured smile,
The value of love and of giving,
The things that make life worthwhile?...
Can you measure the value of friendship,
Of knowing that someone is there,
Of faith and of hope and of courage,
A treasured and goodly share?
For nothing is higher in value,
Whatever life chooses to send—
We must prove that we, too, are worthy
And equal the worth of a friend.

GARNETT ANN SCHULTZ

We must not, in trying to think about how we
can make a big difference, ignore the small daily
differences we can make which, over time, add up
to big differences that we often cannot foresee.

MARIAN WRIGHT EDELMAN

A Blessed Influence

What we feel, think, and do this moment
influences both our present and the future
in ways we may never know.
Begin. Start right where you are.
Consider your possibilities and find inspiration...
to add more meaning and zest to your life.

ALEXANDRA STODDARD

The blossom cannot tell what becomes of its
fragrance as it drifts away, just as no person
can tell what becomes of her influence
as she continues through life.

The fullness of our heart is expressed in
our eyes, in our touch, in what we write,
in what we say, in the way we walk,
the way we receive, the way we need.

MOTHER TERESA

How blessed the man you train, GOD,
the woman you instruct in your Word,
providing a circle of quiet
within the clamor of evil....
God will never walk away from his people,
never desert his precious people.
Rest assured that justice is on its way
and every good heart put right.

PSALM 94:12–15 THE MESSAGE

A mother is not a person to lean on,
but a person to make leaning unnecessary.

DOROTHY CANFIELD FISHER

....

There is no influence so powerful
as that of the mother.

SARAH JOSEPHA HALE

....

The Promise of Faith

If it can be verified, we don't need faith....
Faith is for that which lies on
the other side of reason.
Faith is what makes life bearable, with all its
tragedies and ambiguities and
sudden, startling joys.

MADELEINE L'ENGLE

Faith means being sure of what we hope
for...now. It means knowing something is real,
this moment, all around you, even when you
don't see it. Great faith isn't the ability to believe
long and far into the misty future. It's simply
taking God at His word and taking the next step.

JONI EARECKSON TADA

....

*Faith expects from God what is
beyond all expectations.*

....

Finding acceptance with joy, whatever
the circumstances of life—whether they are
petty annoyances or fiery trials—
this is a living faith that grows.

MARY LOU STEIGLEDER

I pray that Christ will live in your hearts
by faith and that your life will be strong
in love and be built on love.

EPHESIANS 3:17 NCV

I see Heaven's glories shine,
And faith shines equal, arming me from fear.

EMILY BRONTË

True faith drops its letter in the post office box
and lets it go. Distrust holds on to a corner of it
and wonders that the answer never comes.

L. B. COWMAN

Wonderful Peace

We give thanks for the darkness of the night
where lies the world of dreams....
Give us good dreams and memory of them
so that we may carry their poetry
and mystery into our daily lives....
Let us restore the night and reclaim it
as a sanctuary of peace, where silence
shall be music to our hearts and darkness
shall throw light upon our souls.

MICHAEL LEUNIG

O heavenly Father, protect and bless all things
that have breath: guard them from all evil
and let them sleep in peace.

ALBERT SCHWEITZER

Only God gives true peace—a quiet gift
He sets within us just when we think
we've exhausted our search for it.

May God kiss you with His peace,
as a mother kisses her little child.
And may you know that peace isn't
a pot of gold rewarded to you
after chasing some rainbow's end—
it's a gift.

May your footsteps set you upon
a lifetime journey of love.
May you wake each day with His blessings
and sleep each night in His keeping.
And may you always walk in His tender care.

....

*Grace and peace to you from
God our Father and from
the Lord Jesus Christ.*

Romans 1:7 niv

....

God Bless Your Children

I wish I had a box,
the biggest I could find,
I'd fill it right up to the brim
with everything that's kind.
A box without a lock, of course,
and never any key;
for everything inside that box
would then be offered free.
Grateful words for joys received
I'd freely give away.
Oh, let us open wide a box
of praise for every day.

Each day is a treasure box of gifts from God,
just waiting to be opened. Open your gifts
with excitement. You will find forgiveness
attached to ribbons of joy. You will find love
wrapped in sparkling gems.

JOAN CLAYTON

Parents who instruct and nurture their
children in God's ways will see fulfilled
that great promise—"he will not depart from it."

CATHERINE MARSHALL

Just as Jesus took the children,
put His hands on them and blessed them...
we can hold our children in our arms,
touching, blessing, and praying over them.

QUIN SHERRER

*May the LORD richly bless
both you and your children.*

PSALM 115:14 NLT

Bless our children, God, and help us so to
fashion their souls by precept and example
that they may ever love the good,
flee from sin, revere Thy Word,
and honor Thy name.

UNION PRAYER BOOK

Special Gifts We Share

We should make the most of what God gives,
both the bounty and the capacity to enjoy it,
accepting what's given and delighting
in the work. It's God's gift!
God deals out joy in the present, the now.

ECCLESIASTES 5:18 THE MESSAGE

Since you are like no other being ever created
since the beginning of time, you are incomparable.

BRENDA UELAND

God's designs regarding you, and His methods of
bringing about these designs, are infinitely wise.

MADAME JEANNE GUYON

Our greatest responsibility today may be
the unselfish sacrifice of our time, talent, and
love in the lives of those little ones around us.

SUSAN DOWNS

Give, and it will be given to you. A good
measure, pressed down, shaken together and
running over, will be poured into your lap.
For with the measure you use,
it will be measured to you.

LUKE 6:38 NIV

Each one of us is God's special work of art.
Through us, He teaches and inspires, delights
and encourages, informs and uplifts
all those who view our lives.

JONI EARECKSON TADA

....

*God gave me my gifts. I will do all I can
to show Him how grateful I am to Him.*

GRACE LIVINGSTON HILL

....

Wisdom to Live By

At the end of your life you will never regret
not having passed one more test, not winning
one more verdict, or not closing one more deal.
You will regret time not spent with a husband,
a friend, a child, or a parent.

BARBARA BUSH

Whenever I need help being a mother,
I remember my mother and grandmother,
women who planted seeds of wisdom in
my soul, like a secret garden, to flower
even in the bitterest cold.

JUDITH TOWSE-ROBERTS.

Wisdom is knowing the truth, and telling it.

True wisdom and power are found in God;
counsel and understanding are his.

JOB 12:13 NLT

Heavenly Father, please give me wisdom in
daily protecting my children. Whether it's
concerning the people they come in contact with,
the television and videos they watch, or the
many other issues that affect them,
may I be aware of my responsibility
to guide and nurture their minds. Amen.

KIM BOYCE

....

*The wise don't expect to find life worth living;
they make it that way*

....

We ought to be able to learn things secondhand.
There is not enough time for us to make
all the mistakes ourselves.

HARRIET HALL

Teach us to number our days aright,
that we may gain a heart of wisdom.

PSALM 90:12 NIV

Irreplaceable

If God gives such attention to the appearance
of wildflowers—most of which are never
even seen—don't you think he'll attend to you,
take pride in you, do his best for you?

What I'm trying to do here is to get you to
relax, to not be so preoccupied with *getting*,
so you can respond to God's *giving*.
People who don't know God and the way
he works fuss over these things, but you know
both God and how he works.

Steep your life in God-reality,
God-initiative, God-provisions. Don't worry
about missing out. You'll find all your
everyday human concerns will be met.

MATTHEW 6:30-33 *THE MESSAGE*

All that we have and are is one of the unique and
never-to-be-repeated ways God has chosen to
express Himself in space and time. Each of us,
made in His image and likeness, is yet another
promise He has made to the universe that He
will continue to love it and care for it.

BRENNAN MANNING

We have missed the full impact of the Gospel
if we have not discovered what it is to be ourselves,
loved by God, irreplaceable in His sight,
unique among our fellow men.

BRUCE LARSON

....

*Embrace your uniqueness. Time is much too
short to be living someone else's life.*

KOBI YAMADA

....

A Reason for Praise

I have never committed the least matter to God,
that I have not had reason for infinite praise.

ANNA SHIPTON

Dear Heavenly Father, please go with
each member of my family each day.
Protect us as we go our separate ways.
When we meet again, together we will
praise and worship You and give thanks
for Your guidance and protection. Amen.

MARILYN JANSEN

*Sing praises to the Lord,
you who belong to him;
praise his holy name.*

PSALM 30:4 NCV

May your life become one of glad and unending
praise to the Lord as you journey through this
world, and in the world that is to come!

TERESA OF AVILA

Then we, your people, the ones
you love and care for,
will thank you over and over and over.
We'll tell everyone we meet
how wonderful you are,
how praiseworthy you are!

PSALM 79:13 THE MESSAGE

They that trust the Lord find many things to
praise Him for. Praise follows trust.

LILY MAY GOULD

How much of our lives are...well...so daily.
How often our hours are filled with the mundane,
seemingly unimportant things that
have to be done, whether at home or work.
These very "daily" tasks could become
a celebration of praise.
"It is through consecration," someone has said,
"that drudgery is made divine."

GIGI GRAHAM TCHIVIDJIAN

Eternal Moments

Friendships, family ties, the companionship
of little children, an autumn forest flung
in prodigality against a deep blue sky,
the intricate design and haunting fragrance
of a flower, the counterpoint of a Bach fugue
or the melodic line of a Beethoven sonata,
the fluted note of bird song, the glowing
glory of a sunset: the world is aflame
with things of eternal moment.

E. MARGARET CLARKSON

Life is what we are alive to. It is not length but
breadth.... Be alive to...goodness, kindness, purity,
love, history, poetry, music, flowers, stars,
God, and eternal hope.

MALTBIE D. BABCOCK

You have made known to me the path of life;
you will fill me with joy in your presence,
with eternal pleasures at your right hand.

PSALM 16:11 NIV

When we life centered around
what others like, feel and say,
we lose touch with our own identity.
I am an eternal being, created by God.
I am an individual with purpose.
It's not what I get from life, but who I am,
that makes the difference.

NEVA COYLE

....

All that is not eternal is out of date.

C. S. LEWIS

....

Choices can change our lives profoundly.
The choice to mend a broken relationship,
to say "yes" to a difficult assignment, to lay
aside some important work to play with a child,
to visit some forgotten person—these small
choices may affect many lives eternally.

GLORIA GAITHER

My Mother, My Friend

Having someone who understands
is a great blessing for ourselves.
Being someone who understands
is a great blessing to others.

JANETTE OKE

Instant availability without continuous presence
is probably the best role a mother can play.

L. BAILYN

Everyone was meant to share
God's all-abiding love and care;
He saw that we would need to know
a way to let these feelings show....
So God made hugs.

JILL WOLF

....

*We should all have one person who knows
how to bless us despite the evidence.*

PHYLLIS THEROUX

....

Oh, the comfort, the inexpressible comfort
of feeling safe with a person—having neither
to weigh thoughts nor measure words,
but pouring them all right out just as they are,
chaff and grain together, certain that
a faithful hand will take and sift them,
keep what is worth keeping and then,
with the breath of kindness,
blow the rest away.

DINAH MARIA MULOCK CRAIK

Make me very happy by having the same
thoughts, sharing the same love,
and having one mind and purpose.

PHILIPPIANS 2:2 NCV

Listening...means taking a vigorous,
human interest in what is being told us.
You can listen like a blank wall or like
a splendid auditorium where every sound
comes back fuller and richer.

ALICE DUER MILLER

Loved by God

Blue skies with white clouds on summer days.
A myriad of stars on clear moonlit nights. Tulips
and roses and violets and dandelions and daisies.
Bluebirds and laughter and sunshine and Easter.
See how He loves us!

ALICE CHAPIN

We think God's love rises and falls with our
performance. It doesn't.... He loves you for
whose you are: you are His child.

MAX LUCADO

God knows everything about us. And He cares
about everything. Moreover, He can manage
every situation. And He loves us! Surely this is
enough to open the wellsprings of joy....
And joy is always a source of strength.

HANNAH WHITALL SMITH

This is how much God loved the world:
He gave his Son, his one and only Son.
And this is why: so that no one need be
destroyed; by believing in him, anyone can
have a whole and lasting life.

JOHN 3:16 THE MESSAGE

Our greatness rests solely on the fact that
God in His incomprehensible goodness
has bestowed His love upon us. God does not
love us because we are so valuable;
we are valuable because God loves us.

HELMUT THIELICKE

*The Creator thinks enough of you
to have sent Someone very special
so that you might have life—
abundantly, joyfully, completely, and victoriously.*

A Mother's Heart

As a mother comforts her child,
so will I comfort you.

ISAIAH 66:13 NIV

Being a full-time mother is one of
the highest-salaried jobs in any field
since the payment is pure love.

MILDRED B. VERMONT

Women can do no greater thing
than to create the climate of love in their homes.
Love which spoils and pampers,
weakens and hampers.
Real love strengthens and matures
and leaves the loved one free to grow.

EUGENIA PRICE

A mother's love is the heart of the home.
Her children's sense of security and
self-worth are found there.

My mother and I have
laughed over nothing
and cried over everything.
We understand each other's fears,
losses, and sense of humor.
She holds my heart
like no one else can.

JANETTE OKE

You have to love your children unselfishly.
That's hard. But it's the only way.

BARBARA BUSH

Love grows from our capacity to
give what is deepest within ourselves
and also receive what is the deepest
within another person. The heart
becomes an ocean strong and deep,
launching all on its tide.

*No one ever outgrows
the need for a mother's love.*

More to This Life

Life is not intended to be simply a round of work,
no matter how interesting and important that
work may be. A moment's pause to watch the glory
of a sunrise or a sunset is soul satisfying, while
a bird's song will set the steps to music all day long.

LAURA INGALLS WILDER

God desires that the work we do bring us
enduring joy and satisfaction. This will naturally
happen when our efforts are labors of love
that bring Him glory and praise.

BEVERLY LaHAYE

....

*Enjoy the little things. One day
you may look back and realize...
they were the big things.*

....

Why is everyone hungry for more?
"More, more," they say. "More, more."
I have God's more-than-enough,
More joy in one ordinary day
Than they get in all their shopping sprees.
At day's end I'm ready for sound sleep,
For you, God, have put my life back together.

PSALM 4:6–8 THE MESSAGE

If there is a God who speaks anywhere,
surely He speaks here: through waking up and
working, through going away and coming back
again, through people you read and books
you meet, through falling asleep in the dark.

FREDERICK BUECHNER

Get the pattern of your life from God,
then go about your work and be yourself.

PHILLIPS BROOKS

Everyday Miracles

To be alive, to be able to see, to walk,
to have a home, music, paintings, friends—
it's all a miracle. I have adopted the technique
of living life from miracle to miracle.

ARTUR RUBINSTEIN

I think miracles exist in part as gifts
and in part as clues that there is
something beyond the flat world we see.

PEGGY NOONAN

The child must know that he is a miracle,
that since the beginning of the world
there hasn't been, and until the end of the world
there will not be, another child like him.

PABLO CASALS

Open my eyes so I can see
what you show me of your miracle-wonders.

PSALM 119:18 THE MESSAGE

*When we do the best we can, we never
know what miracle is wrought in our life,
or in the life of another.*

HELEN KELLER

We couldn't conceive of a miracle
if none had ever happened.

LIBBIE FUDIM

A gentle word, a kind look, a good-natured smile
can work wonders and accomplish miracles.

WILLIAM HAZLETT

The miracles of nature do not seem miracles
because they are so common. If no one had ever
seen a flower, even a dandelion would be
the most startling event in the world.

Know that you yourself are a miracle.

NORMAN VINCENT PEALE

Encouragement Means So Much

Encouragement is being a good listener,
being positive, letting others know you accept
them for who they are. It is offering hope,
caring about the feelings of
another, understanding.

GIGI GRAHAM TCHIVIDJIAN

Your love has given me much joy
and comfort...for your kindness has often
refreshed the hearts of God's people.

PHILEMON 1:7 NLT

Some days, it is enough encouragement
just to watch the clouds break up and disappear,
leaving behind a blue patch of sky
and bright sunshine that is
so warm upon my face.
It's a glimpse of divinity;
a kiss from heaven.

A word of encouragement to those we meet,
a cheerful smile in the supermarket, a card or
letter to a friend, a readiness to witness
when opportunity is given—all are practical ways
in which we may let His light shine through us.

ELIZABETH B. JONES

Be joyful. Grow to maturity. Encourage each other.
Live in harmony and peace. Then the God of
love and peace will be with you.

2 CORINTHIANS 13:11 NLT

....

*There are times when encouragement means
such a lot. And a word is enough to convey it.*

GRACE STRICKER DAWSON

....

A mother is one who knows you as you
really are, understands where you've been,
accepts who you've become, and
still gently invites you to grow.

Joys of Motherhood

Sense of humor; God's great gift
causes spirits to uplift,
Helps to make our bodies mend;
lightens burdens; cheers a friend;
Tickles children; elders grin
at this warmth that glows within;
Surely in the great hereafter
heaven must be full of laughter!

One of the great joys of motherhood is
the happiness our children bring into
our lives. Let's make the effort to experience
the laughter of childhood with our children.

KIM BOYCE

If they like it, it serves four; otherwise, six.

ELSIE ZUSSMAN

Truth...has got to be concrete.
And there's nothing more concrete than
dealing with babies, burps, bottles and frogs.

JEANE KIRKPATRICK

Now, as always, the most automated appliance
in a household is the mother.

BEVERLY JONES

When children's eyes are smiling
'Tis God's love that's shining through
With glints of joy and laughter
What good medicine for you!

MARGARET FISHBACK POWERS

A good day: When the wheels of your
shopping cart all go in the same direction.

Children seldom misquote you.
They more often repeat word for word
what you shouldn't have said.

MAE MALOO

The surest way of having something done
is to forbid your kids to do it.

....

*A cheerful look brings joy to the heart;
good news makes for good health.*

PROVERBS 15:30 NLT

....

God Loves Our Children

For my dear little child I'd lasso the moon
and give you my love on a silver spoon.
I'd run 'round the world and back again, too,
to grant you the hope of days bright and new.
But all that I have and all that I do
is nothing compared to God's love for you.

Children of the heavenly Father
Safely in His bosom gather;
Nestling bird nor star in heaven
Such a refuge e'er was given.

CAROLINA SANDELL BERG

How great is the love the Father has lavished
on us, that we should be called children of God!
And that is what we are!

1 JOHN 3:1 NIV

God walks with us.... He scoops us up in
His arms or simply sits with us in silent strength
until we cannot avoid the awesome recognition
that yes, even now, He is here.

GLORIA GAITHER

God is so big He can cover the whole
world with His love, and so small
He can curl up inside your heart.

JUNE MASTERS BACHER

....

*After the love of God, a mother's affection
is the greatest treasure here below.*

....

If nothing seems to go my way today,
this is my happiness: God is my
Father and I am His child.

BASILEA SCHLINK

The Richness of Friendship

We are so very rich if we know just a few people
in a way in which we know no others.

CATHERINE BRAMWELL BOOTH

Knowing what to say is not always necessary;
just the presence of a caring friend
can make a world of difference.

SHERI CURRY

Insomuch as any one pushes you nearer to God,
he or she is your friend.

FRENCH PROVERB

If we would build on a sure foundation in
friendship, we must love friends for their sake
rather than for our own.

CHARLOTTE BRONTË

A friend hears the song in my heart and
sings it to me when my memory fails.

Stay true to the Lord. I love you and
long to see you, dear friends,
for you are my joy.

PHILIPPIANS 4:1 NLT

Don't walk in front of me—I may not follow.
Don't walk behind me—I may not lead.
Walk beside me—And just be my friend.

*Treat your friends like family
and your family like friends.*

I am only as strong as the coffee I drink,
the hairspray I use, and the friends I have.

A friend understands what you are trying to say...
even when your thoughts aren't fitting into words.

ANN D. PARRISH

Homegrown Happiness

How necessary it is to cultivate a spirit of joy.
It is a psychological truth that the physical
acts of reverence and devotion make one feel
devout. The courteous gesture increases one's
respect for others. To act lovingly is to begin
to feel loving, and certainly to act joyfully
brings joy to others which in turn makes one
feel joyful. I believe we are called
to the duty of delight.

DOROTHY DAY

Sometimes the laughter in mothering is
the recognition of the ironies and absurdities.
Sometime, though, it's just
pure, unthinking delight.

BARBARA SCHAPIRO

To be able to find joy in another's joy,
that is the secret of happiness.

If children are to keep their inborn sense of wonder...they need the companionship of at least one adult who can share it, rediscovering with them the joy, excitement, and mystery of the world we live in.

RACHEL CARSON

The Lord has filled my heart with joy;
I feel very strong in the Lord....
I am glad because you have helped me!

1 SAMUEL 2:1 NCV

My hope for you today:
A double helping of laughter,
A cup full of love,
A heart brimming with joy!

....

Joy is the feeling of grinning on the inside.

MELBA COLGROVE

....

I Believe

Faith allows us to continually delight in life
since we have placed our needs in God's hands.

JANET WEAVER SMITH

I believe in the sun even if it isn't shining.
I believe in love even when I am alone.
I believe in God even when He is silent.

....

*Within each of us there is an inner place
where the living God Himself longs to dwell,
our sacred center of belief.*

....

Let your roots grow down into him,
and let your lives be built on him.
Then your faith will grow strong in
the truth you were taught, and you will
overflow with thankfulness.

COLOSSIANS 2:7 NLT

Faith is not an effort, a striving,
a ceaseless seeking,
as so many earnest souls suppose,
but rather a letting go,
an abandonment,
an abiding rest in God that nothing,
not even the soul's shortcomings,
can disturb.

Be alert. Continue strong in the faith.
Have courage, and be strong.

1 Corinthians 16:13 NCV

I do not seek to understand that I may believe,
but I believe in order to understand.
For this I believe—that unless I believe,
I should not understand.

Anselm of Canterbury

A Mother's Love

A Mother's love is something
that no one can explain,
It is made of deep devotion
and of sacrifice and pain....
It believes beyond believing
when the world around condemns,
And it glows with all the beauty
of the rarest, brightest gems.

HELEN STEINER RICE

A mother is someone who dreams great dreams
for you, but then she lets you chase the dreams
you have for yourself and loves you just the same.
In the end, she believes in your dreams
as much as you do.

Finally, all of you should be in agreement,
understanding each other, loving each other
as family, being kind and humble.

1 PETER 3:8 NCV

Women know
The way to rear up children (to be just);
They know a simple, merry, tender knack
Of tying sashes, fitting baby-shoes,
And stringing pretty words that make no sense,
And kissing full sense into empty words;
Which things are corals to cut life upon,
Although such trifles.

ELIZABETH BARRETT BROWNING

....

*If there be one thing pure...that can endure,
when all else passes away...it is a mother's love.*

MARCHIONESS DE SPADARA

....

I hope my children look back on today,
And see a mom who had time to play.
There will be years for cleaning and cooking,
For children grow up while we're not looking.

Celebrate the Day

Not every day of our lives is overflowing with
joy and celebration. But there are moments
when our hearts nearly burst
within us for the sheer
joy of being alive. The first sight of our newborn
babies, the warmth of love in another's eyes,
the fresh scent of rain on a hot summer's eve—
moments like these renew in us
a heartfelt appreciation for life.

GWEN ELLIS

Experience God in the breathless wonder and
startling beauty that is all around you.
His sun shines warm upon your face.
His wind whispers in the treetops.
Like the first rays of morning light,
celebrate the start of each day with God.

I will praise You, for You have answered me,
and have become my salvation.

PSALM 118:21 NKJV

Happy people...enjoy the fundamental,
often very simple things of life.... They savor the
moment, glad to be alive, enjoying their work,
their families, the good things around them.
They are adaptable; they can bend with the wind,
adjust to the changes in their times, enjoy the
contest of life.... Their eyes are turned outward;
they are aware, compassionate.
They have the capacity to love.

JANE CANFIELD

....

*We should look for reasons to celebrate—
an A on a paper, even a good hair day.*

PAM FARREL

....

The Blessing of Gratitude

Gratitude unlocks the fullness of life.
It turns what we have into enough, and more....
It can turn a meal into a feast, a house into a home,
a stranger into a friend. Gratitude makes sense of
our past, brings peace for today, and
creates a vision for tomorrow.

MELODY BEATTIE

Feeling grateful or appreciative of someone
or something in your life actually attracts
more of the things that you appreciate and value
into your life. And, the more of your life that you
like and appreciate, the healthier you'll be.

CHRISTIANE NORTHRUP

Were there no God we would be in
this glorious world with grateful hearts
and no one to thank.

CHRISTINA ROSSETTI

Most of the people I know who have
what I want—which is to say, purpose,
heart, balance, gratitude, joy—are people
with a deep sense of spirituality....
They are part of something beautiful.

ANNE LAMOTT

Gratitude is the memory of the heart.

LYDIA MARIA CHILD

Be thankful. Let the word of Christ dwell
in you richly as you teach and admonish
one another with all wisdom, and as you
sing psalms, hymns and spiritual songs
with gratitude in your hearts to God.

COLOSSIANS 3:15-16 NIV

Family Ties

We were a strange little band of characters,
trudging through life sharing diseases and
toothpaste, coveting one another's desserts,
hiding shampoo, borrowing money, locking each
other out of our rooms, inflicting pain and kissing
to heal it in the same instant, loving, laughing,
defending, and trying to figure out the
common thread that bound us all together.

ERMA BOMBECK

Just accept the fact that as long as
you have children in your home,
your house is going to get messy.

LISA WHELCHEL

A family is a group of individuals who are
related to one another by marriage, birth,
or adoption—nothing more, nothing else.
This is not merely human in origin.
It is God's marvelous creation.

JAMES DOBSON

The family is a school of mutual help.
Each member depends on every other....
Each helps the other when and where the help
is most needed. And every word and deed
of unselfish love comes back
in blessings on its author.

T. L. CUYLER

Having three children in three years was
a great pruning experience in my life.
It was God's creative way of putting me in
a situation where I had to learn patience.

CYNTHIA HEALD

*Other things may change us,
but we start and end with family.*

ANTHONY BRANDT

Love each other with genuine affection,
and take delight in honoring each other.

ROMANS 12:10 NLT

Taking Time to Love

Dear Lord, please help me to remember to
take the time to bestow the kisses today
that I want loved ones to remember tomorrow.

JENNIFER THOMAS

Make the most of every opportunity.
Be gracious in your speech. The goal is
to bring out the best in others.

COLOSSIANS 4:5 THE MESSAGE

Mama's order was heavenly. It had to do with
thoroughness...and taking plenty of time.
It had to do with taking plenty of time with me.

SUSANNAH LESSARD

....

*Getting things accomplished isn't nearly
as important as taking time for love.*

JANETTE OKE

....

Take time to notice all the usually unnoticed,
simple things in life. Delight in the never-ending
hope that's available every day!

WENDY MOORE

Time is a very precious gift of God; so precious
that it's only given to us moment by moment.

AMELIA BARR

Live each day the fullest you can,
not guaranteeing there'll be a tomorrow,
not dwelling endlessly on yesterday.

JANE SEYMOUR

Love each other as if your life depended on it.
Love makes up for practically anything.

I PETER 4:8 THE MESSAGE

Whatever you do,
put romance and enthusiasm
into the lives of your children.

MARGARET R. MACDONALD

In God's Care

There will be days which are great and everything
goes as planned. There will be other days when
we aren't sure why we got out of bed. Regardless
of which kind of day it is, we can be assured
that God takes care of our daily needs.

EMILIE BARNES

God is helping me to be content to set certain gifts
on the shelf at present for the sake of my family.
He is teaching me that He is more interested
in what I am than in what I do.

SANDRA K. STRUBHAR

Be still, and in the quiet moments,
listen to the voice of your heavenly Father.
His words can renew your spirit...
no one knows you and your needs like He does.

JANET WEAVER SMITH

You are God's gift to each other
for the living of these days.

RANDY BECTON

Blessed is the person who is too busy to worry
in the daytime and too sleepy to worry at night.

CAROLINE SCHROEDER

....

God...takes care of everyone in time of need.
His love never quits.

PSALM 136:23, 25 THE MESSAGE

....

If you have a special need today, focus your full
attention on the goodness and greatness of
your Father rather than on the size of your need.
Your need is so small compared to
His ability to meet it.

The Blessing of Dreams

It is necessary that we dream now and then.
No one ever achieved anything
from the smallest to the greatest
unless the dream was dreamed first.

LAURA INGALLS WILDER

When you are inspired by a dream,
God has hit the ball into your court.
Now you have to hit it back with commitment.

ROBERT SCHULLER

We need time to dream, time to remember,
and time to reach the infinite. Time to be.

GLADYS TABER

Now to him who is able to do
immeasurably more than all we ask
or imagine, according to his power that is
at work within us, to him be glory.

EPHESIANS 3:20–21 NIV

How could I be anything but quite happy
if I believed always that all the past is forgiven,
and all the present furnished with power,
and all the future bright with hope.

JAMES SMETHAM

Keep thou thy dreams—the tissue of all wings
Is woven first of them; from dreams are made
The precious and imperishable things,
Whose loveliness lives on, and does not fade.

VIRNA SHEARD

....

*Hope is not a dream, but a way of
making dreams become reality.*

L. J. SUENENS

....

Do not pray for dreams equal to your powers.
Pray for powers equal to your dreams.

ADELAIDE ANN PROCTER

The Strength of Family

Family faces are magic mirrors.
Looking at people who belong to us,
we see the past, present, and future.

GAIL LUMET BUCKLEY

As if that weren't enough, you've blessed my family
so that it will continue in your presence always.
Because you have blessed it, GOD,
it's really blessed—blessed for good!

I CHRONICLES 17:16 THE MESSAGE

Call it clan, call it a network, call it a tribe,
call it a family. Whatever you call it,
whoever you are, you need one.

JANE HOWARD

Families give us many things—love and
meaning, purpose and an opportunity to give,
and a sense of humor.

Sooner or later we all discover that the
important moments in life are not the advertised
ones, not the birthdays, the graduations,
the weddings, not the great goals achieved.
The real milestones are less prepossessing.
They come to the door of memory.

SUSAN B. ANTHONY

....

As for me and my family,
we will serve the LORD.

JOSHUA 24:15 NCV

....

The effect of having other interests beyond
those domestic works well. The more one does
and sees and feels, the more one is able to do,
and the more genuine may be one's appreciation
of fundamental things like home, and love,
and understanding companionship.

AMELIA EARHART

Thank You, Lord!

Let us continually offer the sacrifice of praise
to God, that is, the fruit of our lips, giving
thanks to His name. But do not forget to
do good and to share, for with such
sacrifices God is well pleased.

Hebrews 13:15–16 nkjv

Our thanksgiving today should include
those things which we take for granted, and
we should continually praise our God,
who is true to His promise, who has provided
and retained the necessities for our living.

Betty Fuhrman

Thank You, Father, for loving all
the little children of the world—
no matter how old we are.

Marion Bond West

Thank God for dirty dishes;
They have a tale to tell.
While other folks go hungry,
We're eating pretty well.
With home, and health, and happiness,
We shouldn't want to fuss;
For by this stack of evidence,
God's very good to us.

Thanksgiving puts power in living,
because it opens the generators of the heart
to respond gratefully, to receive joyfully,
and to react creatively.

God, of Your goodness give me Yourself,
for You are enough for me.
And only in You do I have everything.

JULIAN OF NORWICH

....

*Every day shared with the ones we love
is a gift for which we are very thankful!*

....

One of a Kind

Everyone has a unique role to fill in the world and
is important in some respect. Everyone, including
and perhaps especially you, is indispensable.

NATHANIEL HAWTHORNE

Though two children have the same parents,
the same values, the same everything, they
turn out different. Isn't that the genius of God?

The value of a person is not measured
on an applause meter; it is measured
in the heart and mind of God.

JOHN FISHER

You have a unique message to deliver, a unique
song to sing, a unique act of love to bestow.
This message, this song, and this act of love have
been entrusted exclusively to the one and only you.

JOHN POWELL

God loves us for ourselves.
He values our love more than He values
galaxies of new created worlds.

A. W. Tozer

Heavenly Father, thank You for the unique
personalities that You have given to each and
every child. Help me to discover each talent and
gift with which You have blessed my children,
and may I learn how to best cultivate
each of the blossoms You have planted
within their souls. Amen.

Kim Boyce

....

*In his grace, God has given us different gifts
for doing certain things well.*

Romans 12:6 nlt

....

Love All Around

There is no need to plead that the love of God
shall fill our hearts as though He were
unwilling to fill us.... Love is pressing around
us on all sides like air. Cease to resist it
and instantly love takes possession.

AMY CARMICHAEL

....

Only He who created the wonders of the world
entwines hearts in an eternal way.

....

The human heart, at whatever age,
opens only to the heart that opens in return.

MARIA EDGEWORTH

Love the Lord God with all your passion and
prayer and intelligence and energy.

MARK 12:30 THE MESSAGE

Nothing can separate you from His love,
absolutely nothing....
God is enough for time,
and God is enough for eternity.
God is enough!

HANNAH WHITALL SMITH

God will never let you be shaken or moved
from your place near His heart.

JONI EARECKSON TADA

Open your hearts to the love God instills.... God
loves you tenderly. What He gives you is not to be
kept under lock and key, but to be shared.

MOTHER TERESA

What we have once enjoyed we can never lose.
All that we love deeply becomes a part of us.

HELEN KELLER

A Guiding Hand

I'll show my children right from wrong,
encourage dreams and hope;
explain respect for others,
while teaching them to cope
with outside pressures, inside fears,
a world that's less than whole;
and through it all I'll nurture
my children's most precious soul!
Though oftentimes a struggle,
this job I'll never trade;
for in my hand tomorrow lives...
a future God has made.

Children need strength to lean on, a shoulder
to cry on, and an example to learn from.

Usually parents who are lucky in the kind of
children they have, have children who are lucky
in the kind of parents they have.

Teach your children why you believe what you believe. Don't ask them to accept your beliefs blindly. Don't be afraid to teach them to think for themselves. God's Word can withstand the test.

PAUL MEIER

The God who made your children will hear your petitions. He has promised to do so. After all, He loves them more than you do.

JAMES DOBSON

What feeling is so nice as a child's hand in yours? So small, so soft and warm, like a kitten huddling in the shelter of your clasp.

MARJORIE HOLMES

....

Children, come and listen to me. I will teach you to worship the LORD.

PSALM 34:11 NCV

....

A Covering of Prayer

I said a prayer for you today
And I know God must have heard,
I felt the answer in my heart
Although He spoke no word.
I asked that He'd be near you
At the start of each new day,
To grant you health and blessings
And friends to share the way.
I asked for happiness for you
In all things great and small,
But it was His loving care
I prayed for most of all.

....

I have not stopped giving thanks for you,
remembering you in my prayers.

EPHESIANS 1:16 NIV

....

When you were small
And just a touch away,
I covered you with blankets
Against the cool night air.
But now that you are tall
And out of reach,
I fold my hands
And cover you with prayer.

DONA MADDUX COOPER

When we call on God, He bends down His
ear to listen, as a father bends down
to listen to his little child.

ELIZABETH CHARLES

Lord, thank You for my children.
Please inspire me with ways to show them
my love and Yours.
I want them to feel appreciated.
I want to help and encourage them....
I want to bless them.

QUIN SHERRER

A Mother's Own Gift

Oh God, You have given me...a life of clay.
Put Your big hands around mine and guide
my hands so that every time I make
a mark on this life, it will be Your mark.

GLORIA GAITHER

You know how to give good gifts to your children.
How much more your heavenly Father will give
good things to those who ask him!

MATTHEW 7:11 NCV

Maybe all I could do was mother.... And yet,
why did I feel so fulfilled when I bedded down
three kids between clean sheets? What if
raising and instilling values in three children
and turning them into worthwhile human beings
would be the most important contribution
I ever made in my lifetime?

ERMA BOMBECK

In the effort to give good and comforting answers
to the young questioners whom we love,
we very often arrive at good and
comforting answers for ourselves.

RUTH GOODE

Whatever job I perform—whether changing
a diaper, closing a deal, teaching a class,
or writing a book—when I meet legitimate
needs, I am carrying on God's work.

KATHY PEEL

I find joy in receiving my children in prayer
as gifts from God. As I do it almost daily,
I find that it enhances my appreciation of
them and my relationship with them.

JACK TAYLOR

. . . .

Life, love, and laughter—
what priceless gifts to give our children.

PHYLLIS CAMPBELL DRYDEN

. . . .

Living for Today

Live for today but hold your hands
open to tomorrow. Anticipate the future
and its changes with joy. There is a seed
of God's love in every event, every
circumstance, every unpleasant situation
in which you may find yourself

BARBARA JOHNSON

Lord...give me the gift of faith to be
renewed and shared with others each day.
Teach me to live this moment only,
looking neither to the past with regret,
nor the future with apprehension.
Let love be my aim and my life a prayer.

ROSEANN ALEXANDER-ISHAM

Forgetting the past and looking forward to what lies ahead, I press on to reach the end of the race and receive the heavenly prize for which God, through Christ Jesus, is calling us.

PHILIPPIANS 3:13-14 NLT

....

Happy is the person who knows what to remember of the past, what to enjoy in the present, and what to plan for the future.

ARNOLD GLASOW

....

Live today! Live fully each moment of today. Trust God to let you work through this moment and the next. He will give you all you need. Don't skip over the painful or confusing moment— even it has its important and rightful place in the day.

God Bless You

I will let God's peace infuse every part of
today. As the chaos swirls and life's demands
pull at me on all sides, I will breathe in God's
peace that surpasses all understanding.
He has promised that He would set within me
a peace too deeply planted to be affected
by unexpected or exhausting demands.

WENDY MOORE

Remember you are very special to God as
His precious child. He has promised to
complete the good work He has begun in you.
As you continue to grow in Him, He will
teach you to be a blessing to others.

GARY SMALLEY AND JOHN TRENT

Lift up your eyes. Your heavenly Father waits to
bless you—in inconceivable ways to make your
life what you never dreamed it could be.

ANNE ORTLUND

A mother is a gift from God
that's blessed in every part...
born through love and loyalty...
conceived within the heart.

No one can fully measure the blessings that come
to the life of the one who has a praying mother.

ROY LESSIN

I thank God, my mother,
for the blessing you are...
for the joy of your laughter...
the comfort of your prayers...
the warmth of your smile.

....

May the LORD, the God of your fathers,
increase you a thousand times and
bless you as he has promised!

DEUTERONOMY 1:11 NIV

....

Light for the Way

A new path lies before us;
We're not sure where it leads;
But God goes on before us,
Providing all our needs.
This path, so new, so different
Exciting as we climb,
Will guide us in His perfect will
Until the end of time.

LINDA MAURICE

I believe that God is in me as the sun is in
the color and fragrance of a flower—the
Light in my darkness, the Voice in my silence.

HELEN KELLER

....

Your word is a lamp to my feet
and a light for my path.

PSALM 119:105 NIV

....

God has not promised skies always blue,
flower-strewn pathways all our lives through;
God has not promised sun without rain,
joy without sorrow, peace without pain.
But God has promised strength for the day,
rest for the labor, light for the way,
grace for the trials, help from above,
unfailing sympathy, undying love.

ANNIE JOHNSON FLINT

Faith in small things has repercussions that
ripple all the way out. In a huge, dark room
a little match can light up the place.

JONI EARECKSON TADA

The light of God surrounds me;
The love of God enfolds me;
The power of God protects me;
The presence of God watches over me.
Wherever I am, God is.

The Lord Is My Strength

The LORD is my strength and my shield;
my heart trusts in him, and I am helped.
My heart leaps for joy and I will
give thanks to him in song.

PSALM 28:7 NIV

God never abandons anyone on whom He
has set His love; nor does Christ, the good
shepherd, ever lose track of His sheep....
We need to "wait upon the Lord"
in meditations on His majesty, till we find
our strength renewed through the
writing of these things upon our hearts.

J. I. PACKER

....

*You have no strength but what God gives and
you can have all the strength that God can give.*

ANDREW MURRAY

....

Lord, let the glow of Your love
Through my whole being shine
Fill me with gladness from above
and hold me by strength Divine.

MARGARET FISHBACK POWERS

God's love is like a river springing up in
the Divine Substance and flowing endlessly
through His creation, filling all things
with life and goodness and strength.

THOMAS MERTON

Should we feel at times disheartened and
discouraged, a simple movement of heart toward
God will renew our powers. Whatever He may
demand of us, He will give us at the moment
the strength and courage that we need.

FRANÇOIS FÉNELON

Friends Make a Difference

To have someone who wants to absorb us,
who wants to understand the shape and structure
of our lives, who will listen for more than our
words, is one of friendship's greatest gifts.

PAUL D. ROBBINS

Good communication is stimulating as black
coffee, and just as hard to sleep after.

ANNE MORROW LINDBERGH

The friend who is really worth having
is the one who will listen to your deepest
hurts and feel they are hers too.

Many women...have buoyed me up
in times of weariness and stress.
Each friend was important....
Their words have seasoned my life.
Influence, just like salt shaken out,
is hard to see, but its flavor is hard to miss.

PAM FARREL

Nature loves nothing solitary, and always reaches
out to something, as a support, which ever
in the sincerest friend is most delightful.

CICERO

....

*Friendship is the fruit gathered from the trees
planted in the rich soil of love, and nurtured
with tender care and understanding.*

ALMA L. WEIXELBAUM

....

Friendship is like love at its best: not blind but
sympathetically all-seeing; a support which
does not wait for understanding; an act of faith
which does not need, but always has, reason.

LOUIS UNTERMEYER

A friend loves at all times,
and a brother is born for adversity.

PROVERBS 17:17 NIV

My Heart Is Content

I am still determined to be cheerful and happy,
in whatever situation I may be;
for I have also learned from experience that
the greater part of our happiness or misery
depends upon our dispositions,
and not upon our circumstances.

MARTHA WASHINGTON

When we put people before
possessions in our hearts,
we are sowing seeds of enduring satisfaction.

BEVERLY LAHAYE

God bless you and utterly satisfy
your heart...with Himself.

AMY CARMICHAEL

Contentment is not the fulfillment
of what you want, but the realization of
how much you already have.

My heart is content with just knowing
The treasures of life's little things;
The thrill of a child when it's snowing,
The trill of a bird in the spring.
My heart is content with just knowing
Fulfillment that true friendship brings;
It fills to the brim, overflowing
With pleasure in life's "little things."

JUNE MASTERS BACHER

Where the soul is full of peace and joy,
outward surroundings and circumstances are of
comparatively little account.

HANNAH WHITALL SMITH

Love, consolation and peace bloom only
in the garden of sweet contentment.

MARTHA ANDERSON

If you're content to simply be yourself,
your life will count for plenty.

MATTHEW 23:11 THE MESSAGE

Praise and Adoration

It's who you are and the way you live that
count before God. Your worship must engage
your spirit in the pursuit of truth. That's the
kind of people the Father is out looking for:
those who are simply and honestly themselves
before him in their worship. God is sheer
being itself—Spirit. Those who worship him
must do it out of their very being, their spirits,
their true selves, in adoration.

JOHN 4:23-24 THE MESSAGE

We can go through all the activities of our
days in joyful awareness of God's presence
with whispered prayers of praise and adoration
flowing continuously from our hearts.

RICHARD J. FOSTER

It is right and good that we, for all things,
at all times, and in all places, give thanks and
praise to You, O God. We worship You, we
confess to You, we praise You, we bless You,
we sing to You, and we give thanks to You:
Maker, Nourisher, Guardian, Healer,
Lord, and Father of all.

LANCELOT ANDREWS

....

Love wholeheartedly, be surprised,
give thanks and praise—then you will
discover the fullness of your life.

DAVID STEINDL-RAST

....

Walk and talk and work and laugh with your
friends, but behind the scenes, keep up the life
of simple prayer and inward worship.

THOMAS R. KELLY

Living in Truth

Open my eyes that I may see
Glimpses of truth Thou hast for me.
Place in my hands the wonderful key
That shall unclasp and set me free:
Silently now I wait for Thee,
Ready, my God, Thy will to see;
Open my eyes, illumine me,
Spirit divine!

CLARA H. SCOTT

....

Truth is always exciting. Speak it, then.
Life is dull without it.

PEARL S. BUCK

....

Anyone who examines this evidence
will come to stake his life on this:
that God himself is the truth.

JOHN 3:31 THE MESSAGE

To follow truth as blind men long for light,
To do my best from dawn of day till night,
To keep my heart fit for His holy sight,
And answer when He calls.
This is my task.

MAUDE LOUISE RAY

Jesus answered,
"I am the way and the truth and the life.
No one comes to the Father except through me."

JOHN 14:6 NIV

I am amazed by the sayings of Christ.
They seem truer than anything I have ever read.
And they certainly turn the world upside down.

KATHERINE BUTLER HATHAWAY

For the Children

There is no greater pleasure than bringing
to the uncluttered, supple mind of a child the
delight of knowing God and the many rich
things He has given us to enjoy.

GLADYS M. HUNT

There are two lasting bequests
we can give our children.
One of these is roots; the other, wings.

HODDING CARTER

A child is a handful some of the time,
but a heartful all of the time.

It's not what you think that influences your child;
it's what you communicate.

CHARLES STANLEY

The time needed to talk to a child, time given
to an impulse—only you can measure the value.
For whatever ways you spend your time,
it ought to pay high dividends in meeting
physical needs and enriching the mind
and spirit of each family member.

ALICE SKELSEY

Recognizing the good in children is one of
the greatest gifts we can give to them.

We will not hide these truths from our children;
we will tell the next generation
about the glorious deeds of the LORD,
about his power and his mighty wonders.

PSALM 78:4 NLT

....

The best gift you can give a child is love.

....

At Mother's Knee

God, help me to be honest
so my children will learn honesty.
Help me to be kind
so my children will learn kindness.
Help me to be faithful
so my children will learn faith.
Help me to love
so that my children will be loving.

MARIAN WRIGHT EDELMAN

If our kids are going to make
an impact in the world,
they must understand God's Word.

LISA WHELCHEL

....

*Train children to live the right way, and
when they are old, they will not stray from it.*

PROVERBS 22:6 NCV

....

Whether we are poets or parents or
teachers or artists or gardeners, we must
start where we are and use what we have.
In the process of creation and relationship,
what seems mundane and trivial may show itself
to be holy, precious, part of a pattern.

LUCI SHAW

To discipline a child produces wisdom....
Discipline your children, and they will give you
peace of mind and will make your heart glad.

PROVERBS 29:15, 17 NLT

The most important thing she'd
learned over the years
was that there was no way to be a perfect mother
and a million ways to be a good one.

JILL CHURCHILL

Little Acts of Kindness

Kindness is the only service that will
stand the storm of life and not wash out.
It will wear well and be remembered
long after the prism of politeness or the
complexion of courtesy has faded away.

Little acts of kindness which we render
to each other in everyday life, are like
flowers by the way-side to the traveler:
they serve to gladden the heart and
relieve the tedium of life's journey.

EUNICE BATHRICK

Little drops of water,
Little grains of sand,
Make the mighty ocean
And the pleasant land.
Little deeds of kindness,
Little words of love,
Help to make earth happy
Like the heaven above.

JULIA FLETCHER CARNEY

Notice words of compassion.
Seek out deeds of kindness.
These are like the doves from heaven,
pointing out to you who are the ones
blessed with inner grace and beauty.

Christopher de Vinck

If you can help anybody even a little,
be glad; up the steps of usefulness and
kindness, God will lead you on to
happiness and friendship.

Maltbie D. Babcock

....

*The older you get the more you realize
that kindness is synonymous with happiness.*

Lionel Barrymore

....

Be kind to one another, tenderhearted,
forgiving one another, even as
God in Christ forgave you.

Ephesians 4:32 nkjv

Through the Eyes of a Child

My child took a crayon
In her little hand
And started to draw
As if by command.

I looked on with pleasure
But couldn't foresee
What the few simple lines
Were going to be.

What are you drawing?
I asked, by and by.
I'm making a picture
Of God in the sky.

But nobody knows
What God looks like, I sighed.
They will when I'm finished
She calmly replied.

SHERWIN KAUFMAN

The most successful parents are those who
have the skill to get behind the eyes of a child,
seeing what they see, thinking what they think,
feeling what they feel.

JAMES DOBSON

Jesus said, "Let the little children come to me,
and do not hinder them, for the kingdom
of heaven belongs to such as these."

MATTHEW 19:14 NIV

In order to manage children well,
we must borrow their eyes and their hearts,
see and feel as they do, and judge them
from their own point of view.

EUGÉNIE DE GUÉRIN

....

*It is a special gift to be able to view the world
through the eyes of a child.*

....

The Gift of Simplicity

Don't ever let yourself get so busy
that you miss those little but important extras
in life—the beauty of a day...the smile of a friend...
the serenity of a quiet moment alone.
For it is often life's smallest pleasures and
gentlest joys that make the biggest
and most lasting difference.

It doesn't take monumental feats to make the
world a better place. It can be as simple as letting
someone go ahead of you in a grocery line.

BARBARA JOHNSON

Let us consider how we may spur one another on
toward love and good deeds.

HEBREWS 10:24 NIV

Simplicity will enable you to leap lightly.
Increasingly you will find yourself living in a
state of grace, finding...the sacred in the ordinary,
the mystical in the mundane.

DAVID YOUNT

A devout life does bring wealth,
but it's the rich simplicity of being yourself
before God. Since we entered the world penniless
and will leave it penniless, if we have bread
on the table and shoes on our feet,
that's enough.

1 TIMOTHY 6:6-8 THE MESSAGE

....

*It isn't the great big pleasures
that count the most; it's making a great deal
out of the little ones.*

JEAN WEBSTER

....

Taking Care of Mom

Though motherhood is the most important of all
the professions—requiring more knowledge than
any other department in human affairs—there was
no attention given to preparation for this office.

ELIZABETH CADY STANTON

Prayer of a young child: "Bless my mommy and
daddy...and dear God, take good care of Yourself.
If anything happens to You, we're sunk."

As a mother, my job is to take care of what is
possible and trust God with the impossible.

RUTH BELL GRAHAM

Part of the curse of motherhood is never knowing
if you're doing a good job. But part of the joy
is realizing no one's really keeping score.

DALE HANSON BOURKE

Motherhood is...the biggest on-the-job
training program in existence today.

ERMA BOMBECK

More so than any other human relationship,
in fact, overwhelmingly more, motherhood
means being instantly interruptible,
responsive, and responsible.

Mother had a thousand thoughts to
get through within a day, and...most of these
were about avoiding disaster.

NATALIE KUSZ

*The real secret behind motherhood...
love, the thing that money can't buy.*

ANNA CROSBY

Cast your cares on the Lord
and he will sustain you.

PSALM 55:22 NIV

Close to Him

Incredible as it may seem, God wants our
companionship. He wants to have us close to Him.
He wants to be a father to us, to shield us,
to protect us, to counsel us, and to guide us
in our way through life.

BILLY GRAHAM

It is good for me to draw near to God;
I have put my trust in the Lord GOD.

PSALM 73:28 NKJV

God still draws near to us in the ordinary,
commonplace, everyday experiences and places....
He comes in surprising ways.

HENRY GARIEPY

It is when things go wrong,
when good things do not happen,
when our prayers seem to have been lost,
that God is most present.

MADELEINE L'ENGLE

The sunshine dancing on the water, the
lulling sound of waves rolling into the shore,
the glittering stars against the night sky—
all God's light, His warmth, His majesty—
our Father of light reaching out to us,
drawing each of us closer to Himself.

WENDY MOORE

*Draw near to God and
He will draw near to you.*

JAMES 4:7 NKJV

By putting the gift of yearning for God
into every human being's heart,
God at the same time draws all people
made in God's image to God's self
and into their own true selves.

ROBERTA BONDI

A Generous Spirit

Love in the heart wasn't put there to stay;
love isn't love 'til you give it away.

OSCAR HAMMERSTEIN II

If your gift is to encourage others,
be encouraging. If it is giving, give
generously.... Don't just pretend
to love others. Really love them.

ROMANS 12:8-9 NLT

The fountain of beauty is the heart,
and every generous thought illustrates
the walls of your chamber.

FRANCIS QUARLES

Don't just get older, get better. Live
realistically. Give generously. Adapt willingly.
Trust fearlessly. Rejoice daily.

CHARLES SWINDOLL

Be happy with what you have and are,
be generous with both, and you
won't have to hunt for happiness.

WILLIAM E. GLADSTONE

Giving is the secret of a healthy life...not
necessarily money, but whatever one has of
encouragement and sympathy and understanding.

JOHN D. ROCKEFELLER JR.

....

*Love is not the saying of the words
but the giving of the self.*

ROBERT LANDER

....

Love is not getting, but giving.... It is goodness
and honor and peace and pure living—
yes, love is that and it is the best thing in the world
and the thing that lives the longest.

HENRY VAN DYKE

A Beautiful Life

Something deep in all of us yearns
for God's beauty, and we can find it
no matter where we are.

SUE MONK KIDD

Consider the lilies, how they grow;
they neither toil nor spin; and yet I say to you,
even Solomon in all his glory was not arrayed
like one of these. If then God so clothes the grass,
which today is in the field and
tomorrow is thrown into the oven,
how much more will He clothe you?

LUKE 12:27-28 NKJV

Isn't it a wonderful morning?
The world looks like something
God had just imagined for His own pleasure.

LUCY MAUD MONTGOMERY

Beauty puts a face on God.
When we gaze at nature, at a loved one,
at a work of art, our soul immediately recognizes
and is drawn to the face of God.

MARGARET BROWNLEY

Every time you smile at someone,
it is an action of love,
a gift to that person, a beautiful thing.

MOTHER TERESA

The Lord is all I need. He takes care of me.
My share in life has been pleasant;
my part has been beautiful.

PSALM 16:5–6 NCV

You are God's created beauty and the
focus of His affection and delight.

JANET WEAVER SMITH

*May God give you eyes to see beauty
only the heart can understand.*

Providing All Our Needs

I must simply be thankful, and I am, for
all the Lord has provided for me, whether
big or small in the eyes of someone else.

MABEL P. ADAMSON

You can trust God right now
to supply all your needs for today.
And if your needs are more tomorrow,
His supply will be greater also.

Throughout the Bible,
when God asked someone to do something,
methods, means, materials and specific
directions were always provided.
That person had one thing to do: obey.

ELISABETH ELLIOT

Provide me with the insight
that comes only from your Word.

PSALM 119:169 THE MESSAGE

Those who know God as their Father know the whole secret. They are His heirs, and may enter now into possession of all that is necessary for their present needs.

HANNAH WHITALL SMITH

It is not my business to think about myself. My business is to think about God. It is for God to think about me.

SIMONE WEIL

You care for the land and water it; you enrich it abundantly. The streams of God are filled with water to provide the people with grain, for so you have ordained it.

PSALM 65:9 NIV

....

God's gifts make us truly wealthy.
His loving supply never shall leave us wanting.

BECKY LAIRD

....

Childhood Memories

There is nothing higher and stronger and
more wholesome and useful for life in later years
than some good memory, especially a memory
connected with childhood, with home.

FYODOR DOSTOYEVSKY

There was a place in childhood
that I remember well,
And there a voice of sweetest tone
bright fairy tales did tell.

SAMUEL LOVER

A family is a "gallery of memories" to those
who have been blessed by the presence of children.

JAMES DOBSON

How dear to the heart are the scenes
of my childhood, when fond recollection
presents them to view.

SAMUEL WOODWORTH

O Lord, you alone are my hope
I've trusted you, O LORD, from childhood.
Yes, you have been with me from birth;
from my mother's womb you have cared for me.
No wonder I am always praising you!
My life is an example to many,
because you have been my strength and protection.
That is why I can never stop praising you;
I declare your glory all day long.

PSALM 71:5-8 NLT

Take the gift of this moment and
make something beautiful of it.
Few worthwhile experiences just happen,
memories are made on purpose.

GLORIA GAITHER

*Memory is the treasury and
guardian of all things.*

CICERO

Be Encouraged

Hope begins in the dark, the stubborn hope
that if you just show up and try to do
the right thing, the dawn will come.
You wait and watch and work:
You don't give up.

ANNE LAMOTT

I'm sure now I'll see God's goodness in the
exuberant earth. Stay with GOD!
Take heart. Don't quit.

PSALM 27:13 THE MESSAGE

God, bless all young mothers at end of day.
Kneeling wearily with each small
one to hear them pray.
Too tired to rise when done...and yet they do;
longing just to sleep one whole night through.
Too tired to sleep.... Too tired to pray....
God, bless all young mothers at close of day.

RUTH BELL GRAHAM

Being taken for granted can be a compliment.
It means that you've become a comfortable,
trusted person in another person's life.

JOYCE BROTHERS

Calm me, O Lord, as You stilled the storm,
Still me, O Lord, keep me from harm.
Let all the tumult within me cease,
Enfold me, Lord, in Your peace.

CELTIC TRADITIONAL

....

*At night I turn my problems over to God.
He's going to be up all night anyway.*

CARRIE WESTINGSON

....

The Scriptures give us hope
and encouragement as we wait patiently
for God's promises to be fulfilled.

ROMANS 15:4 NLT

*W*hen you have laboriously
accomplished your daily task, go to
sleep in peace. God is awake.

VICTOR HUGO